# ISRAEL

PHOTOGRAPHS BY ELIZABETH KRAMER



THIS IS PART OF THE VISITING SERIES.

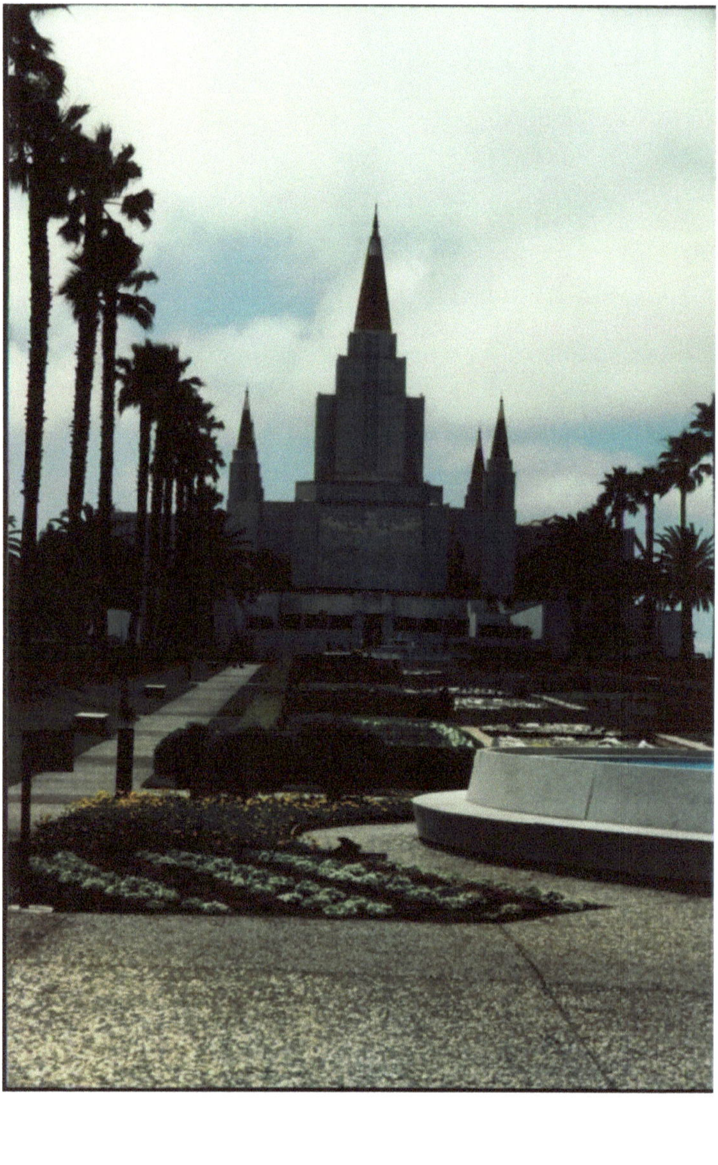

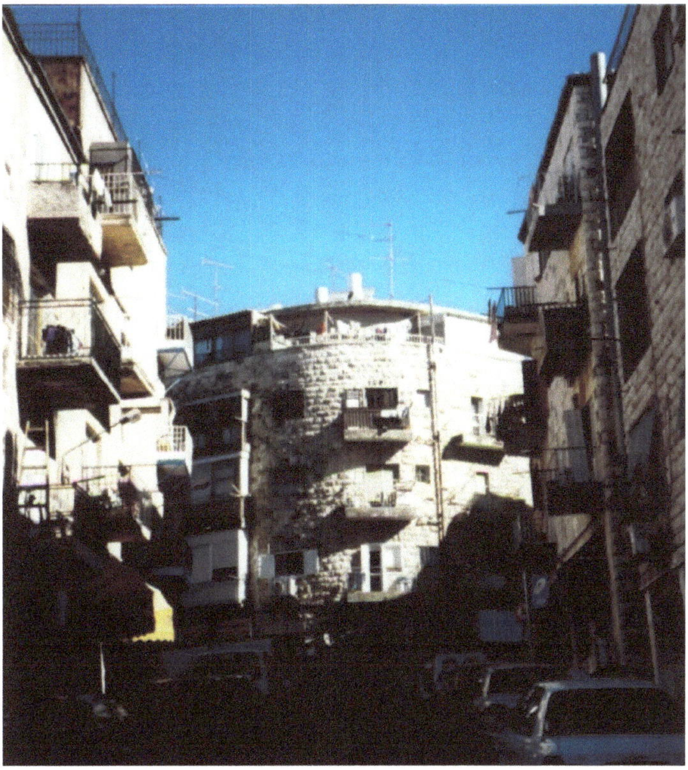

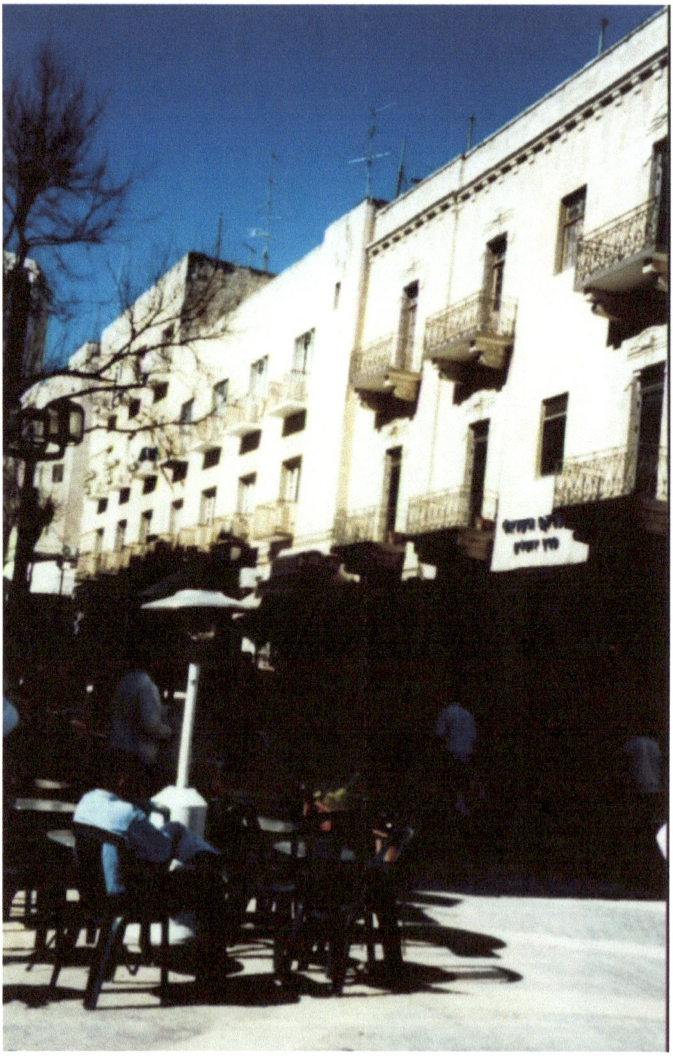

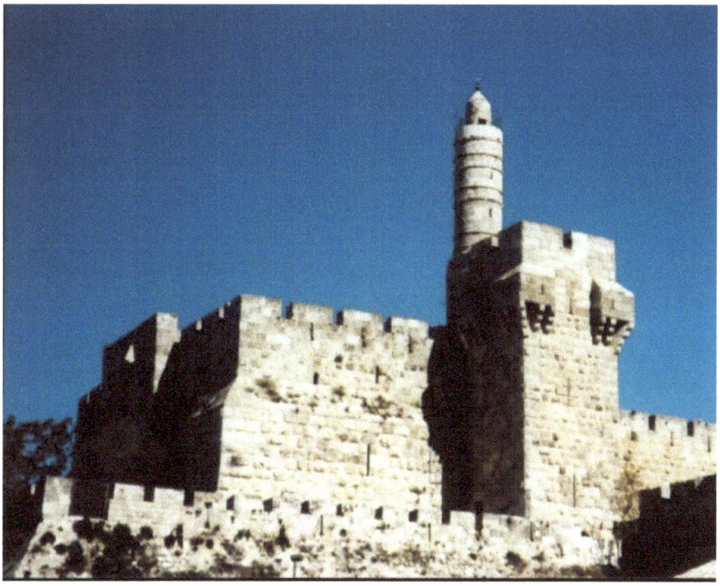

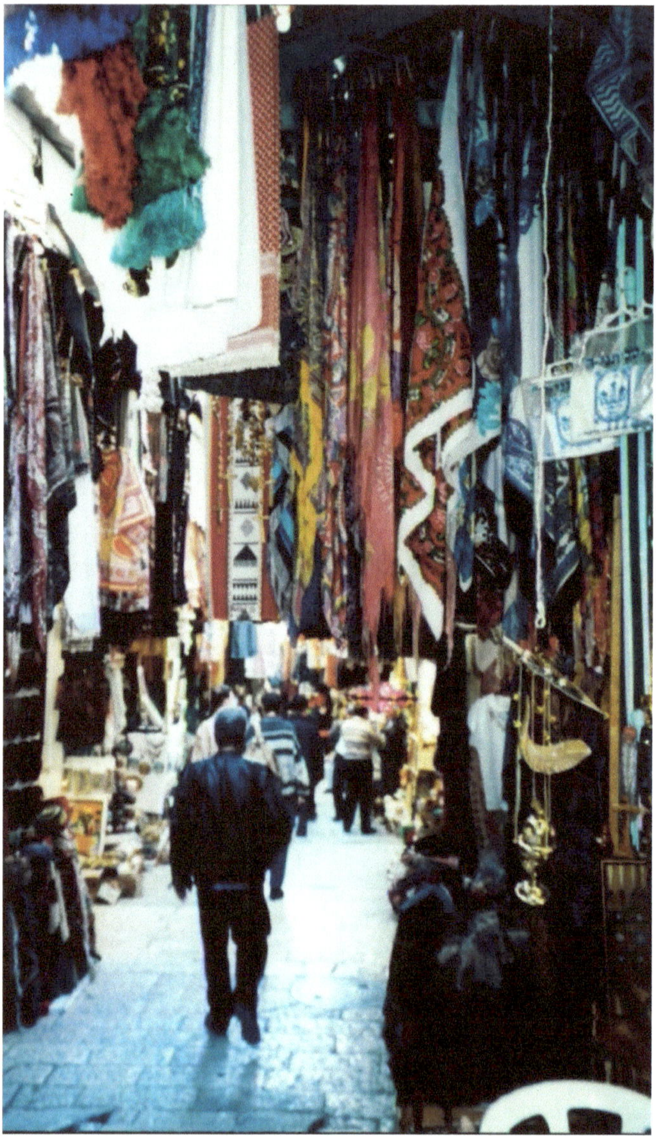

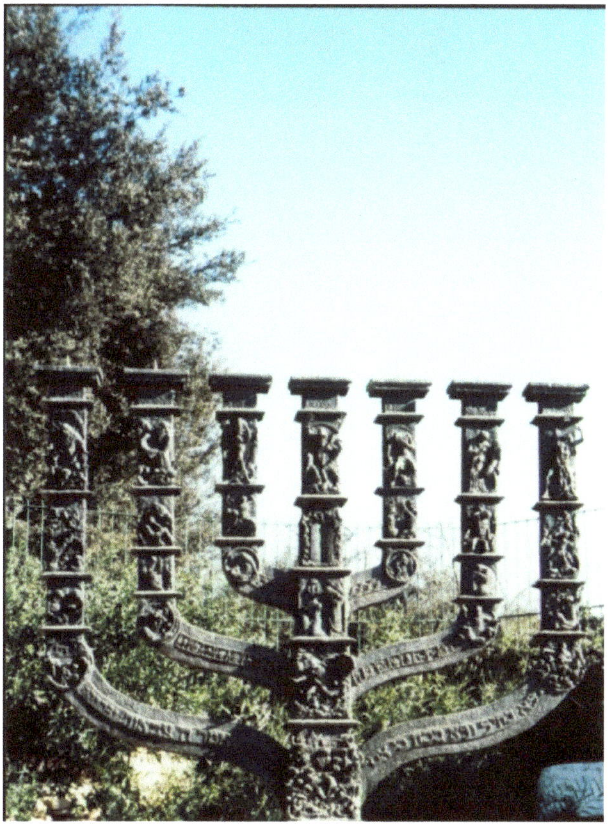

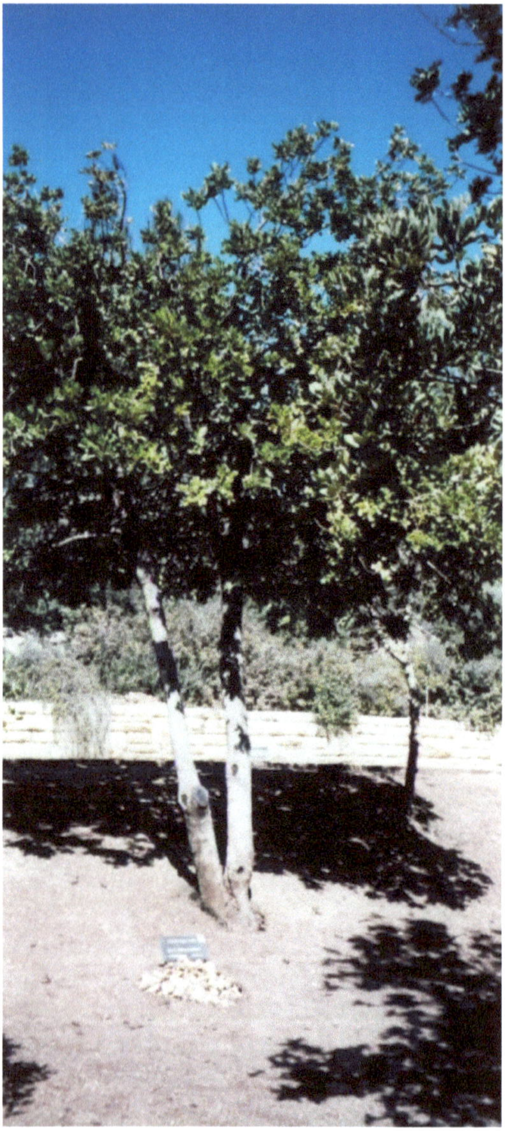

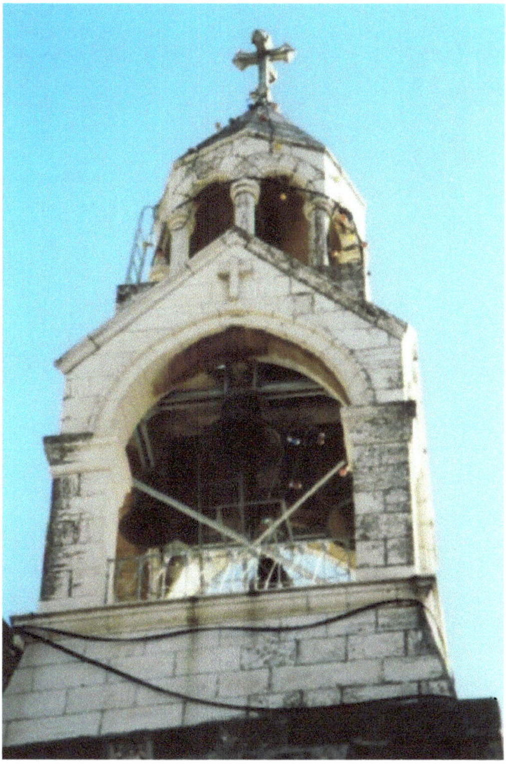

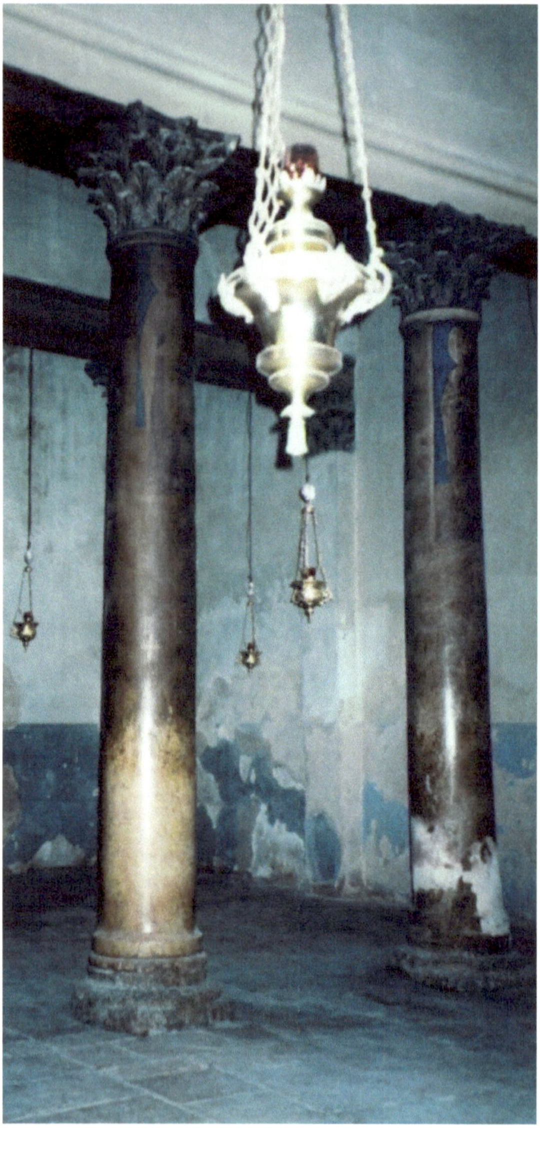

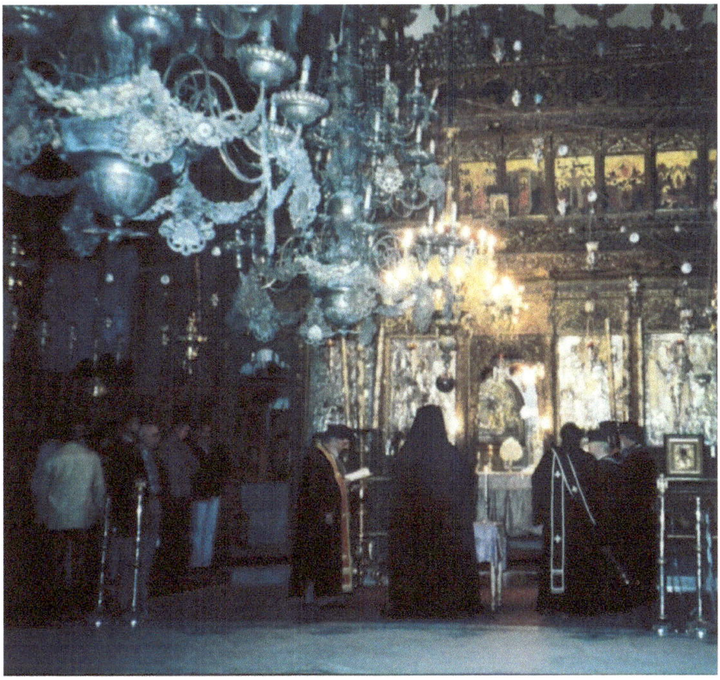

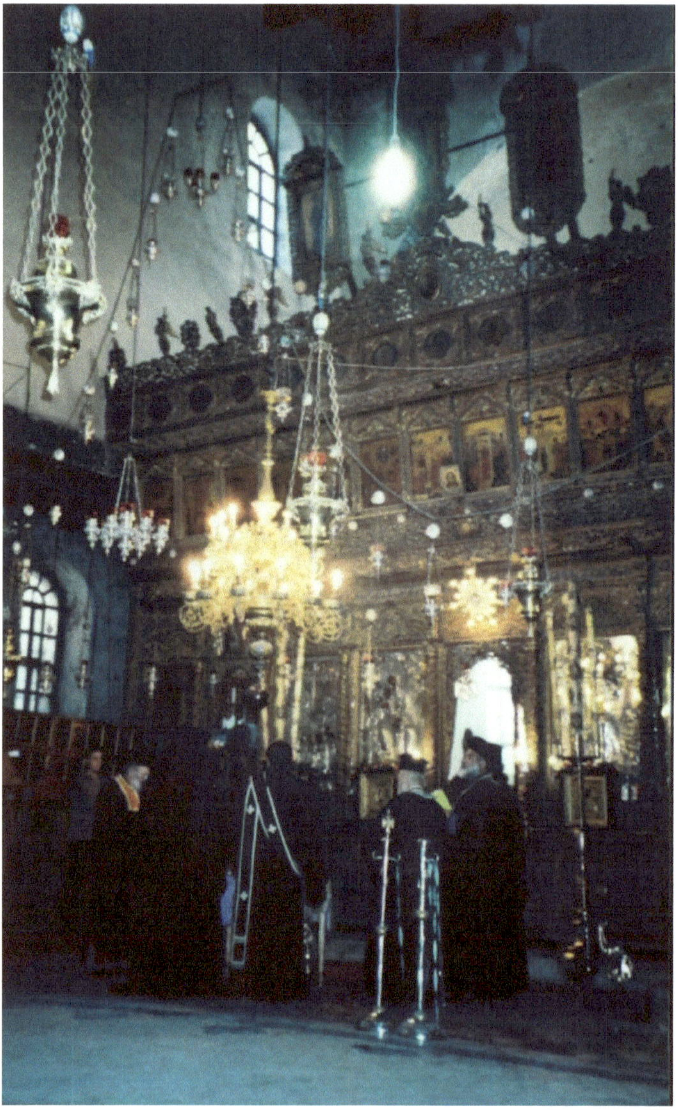

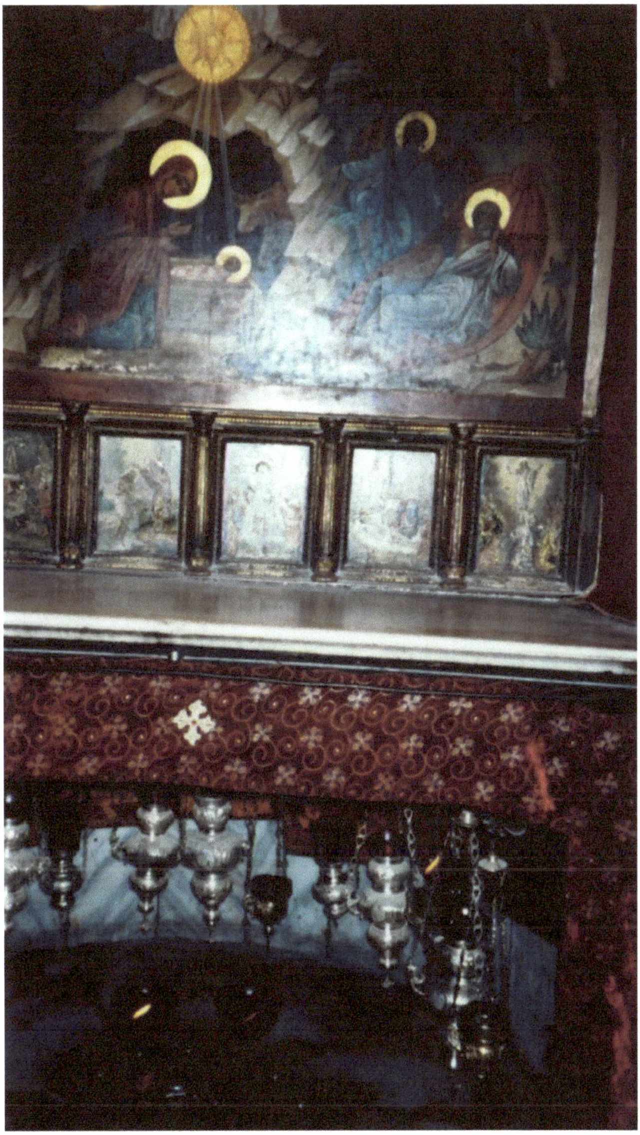

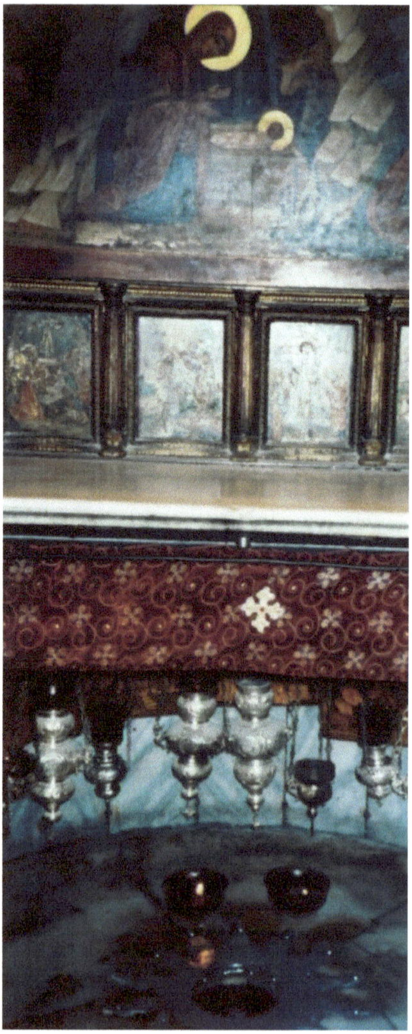

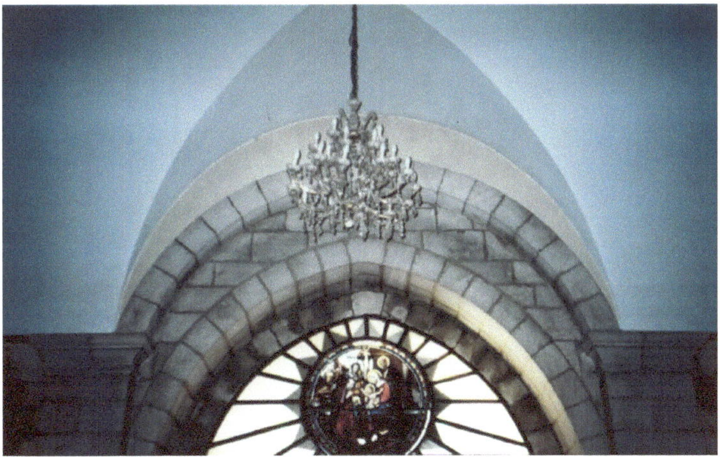

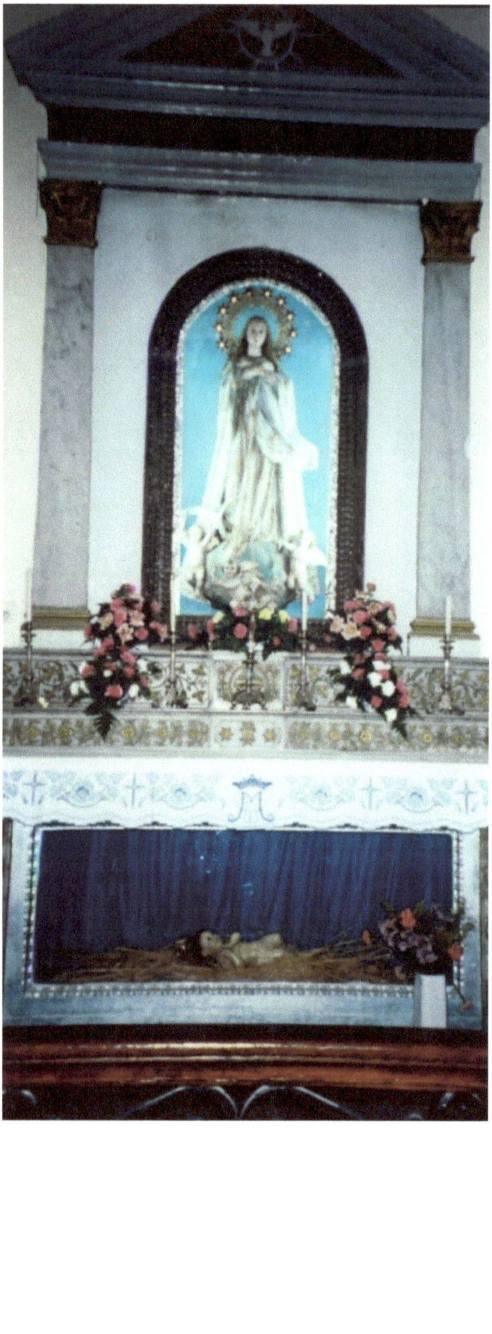

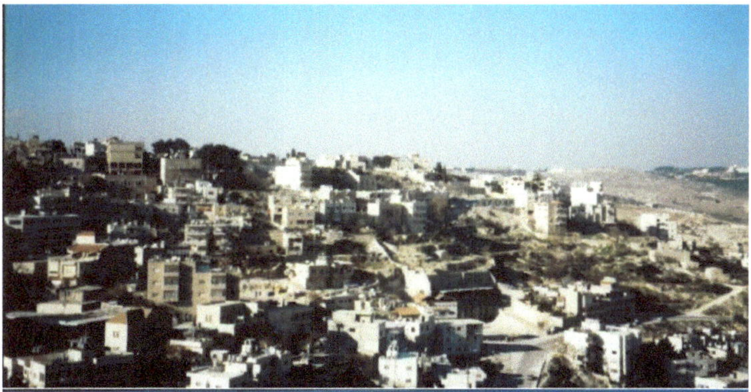

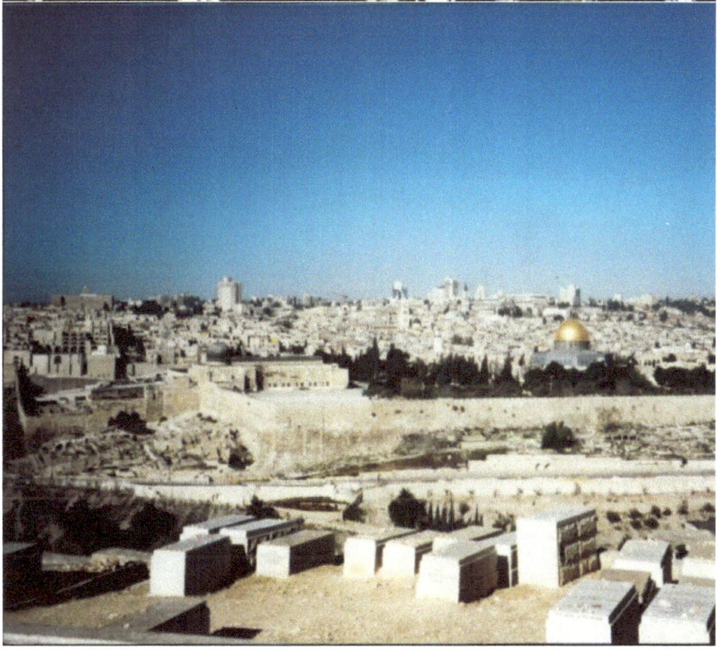

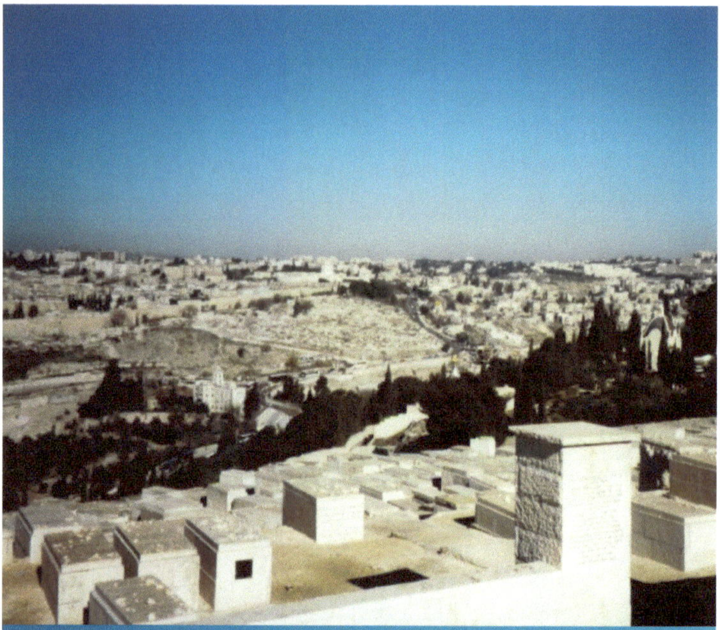

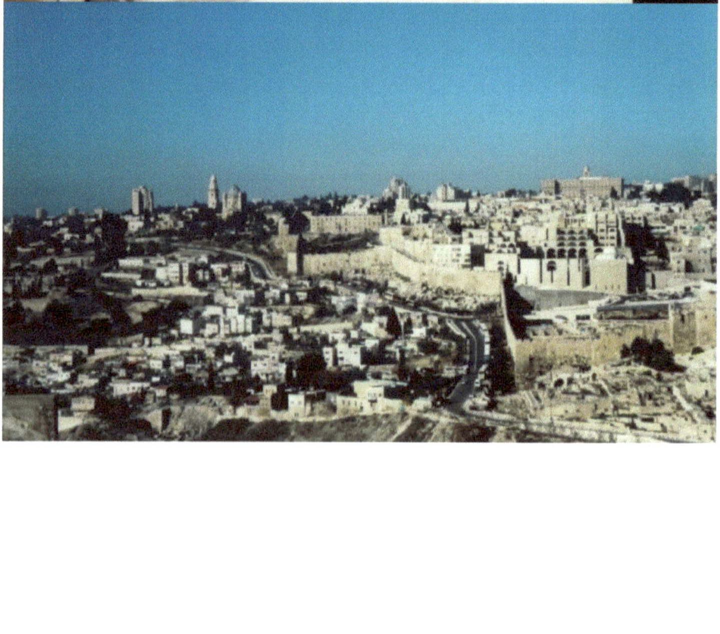

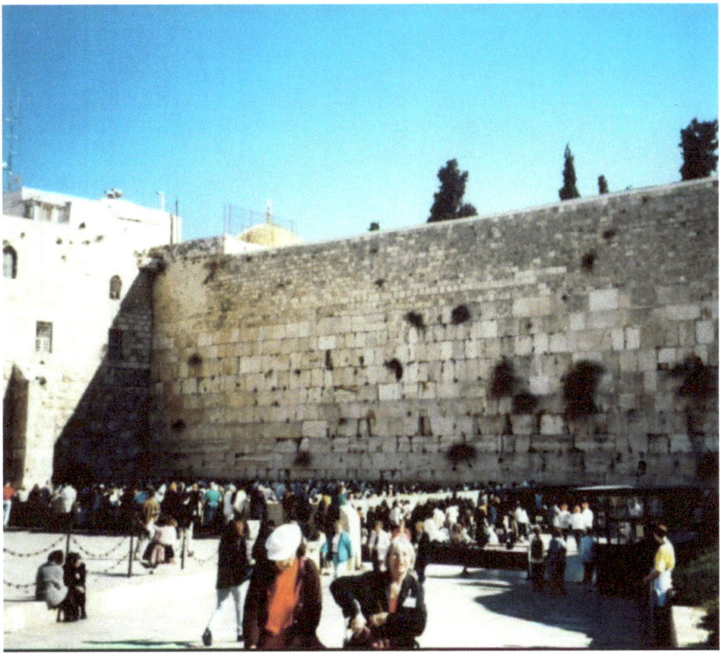

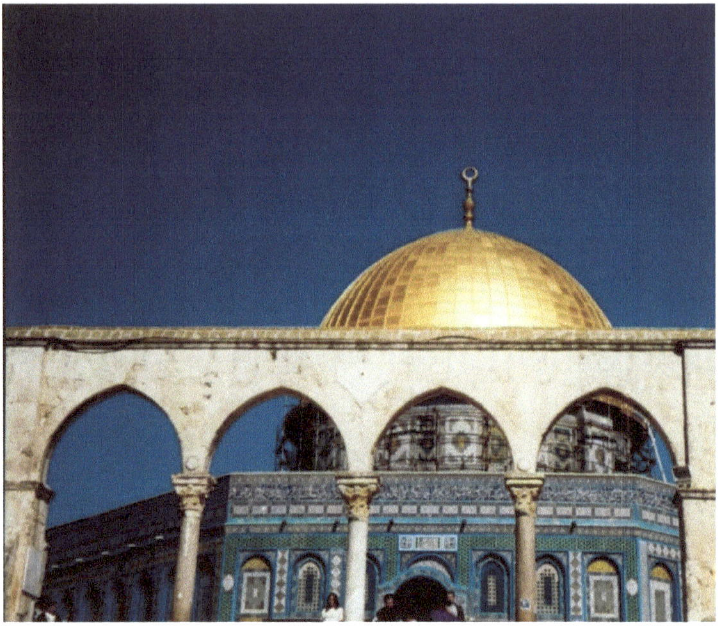

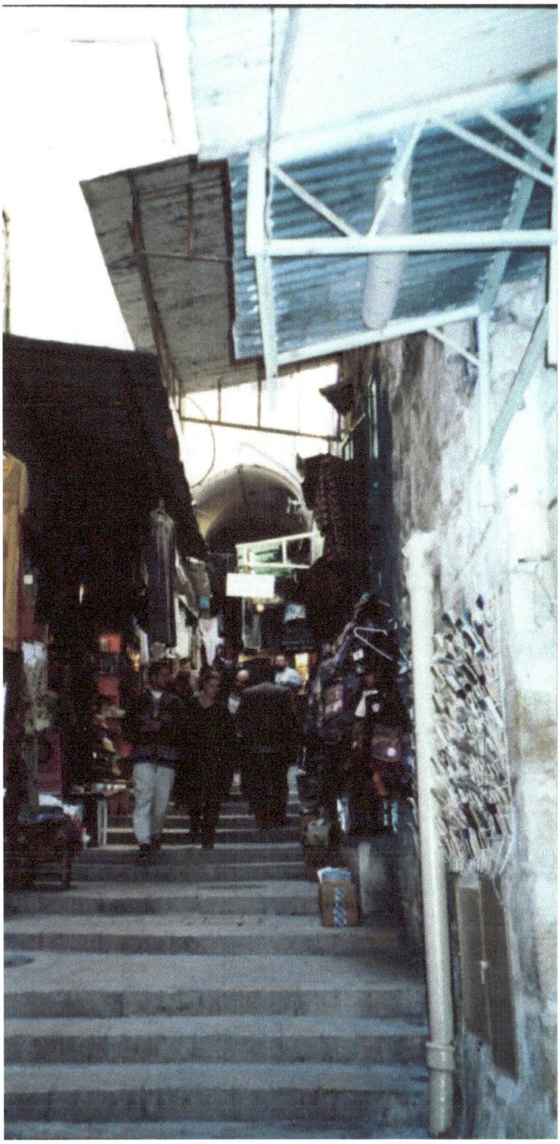

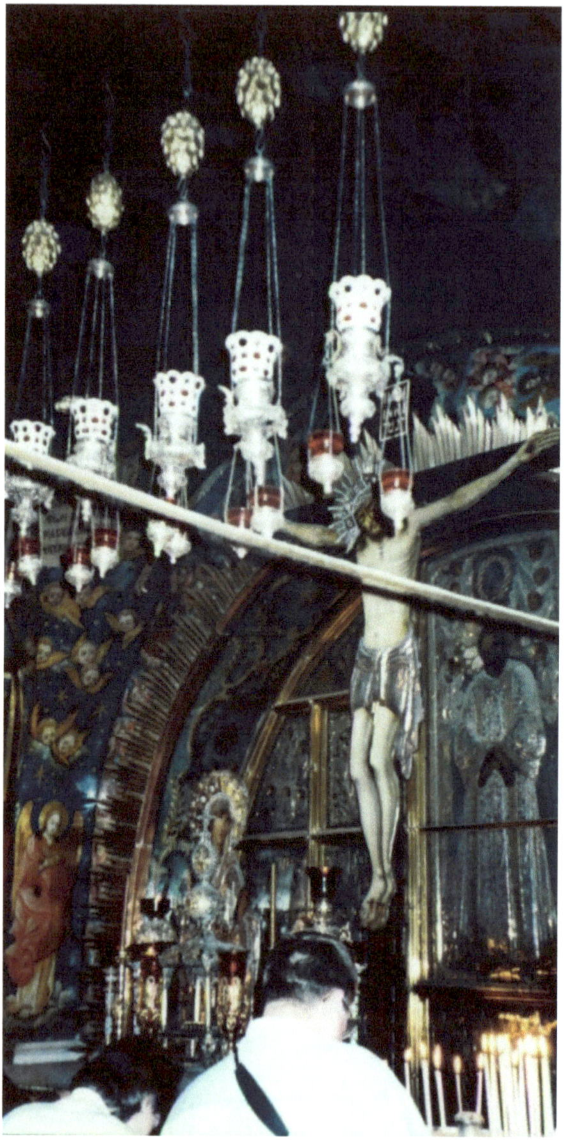

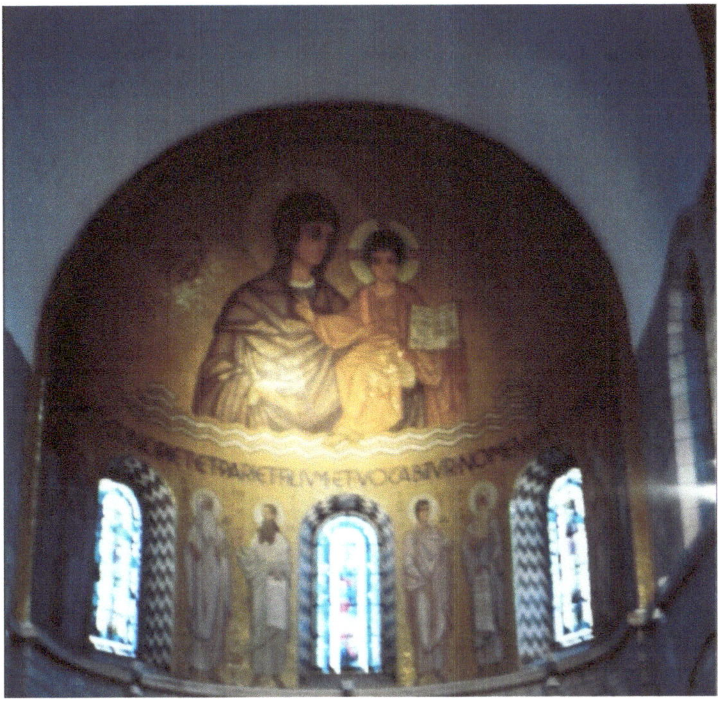

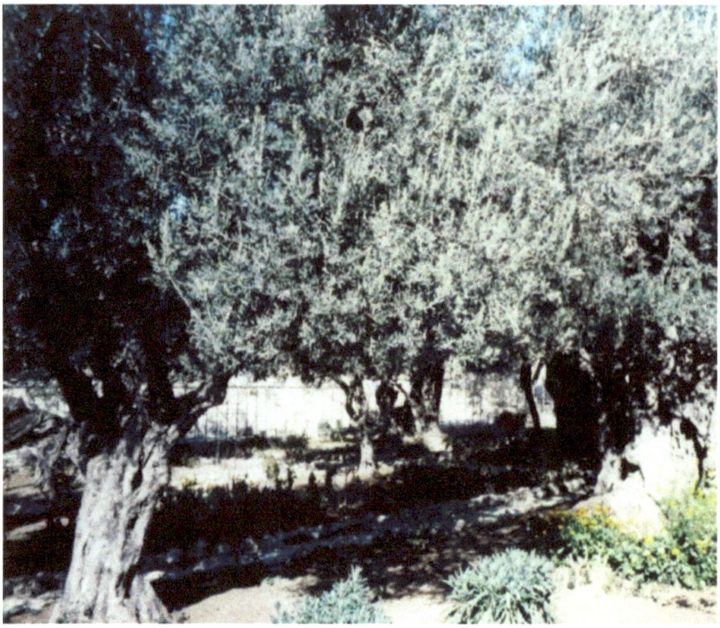

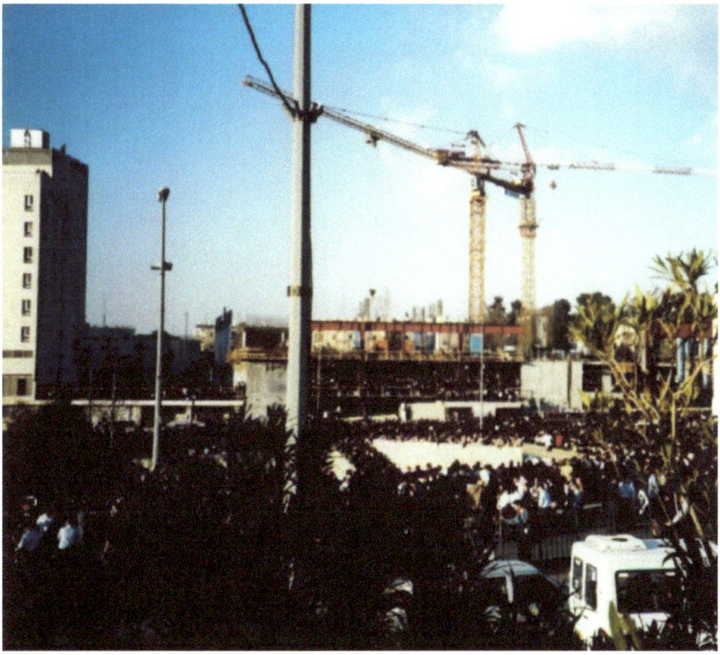

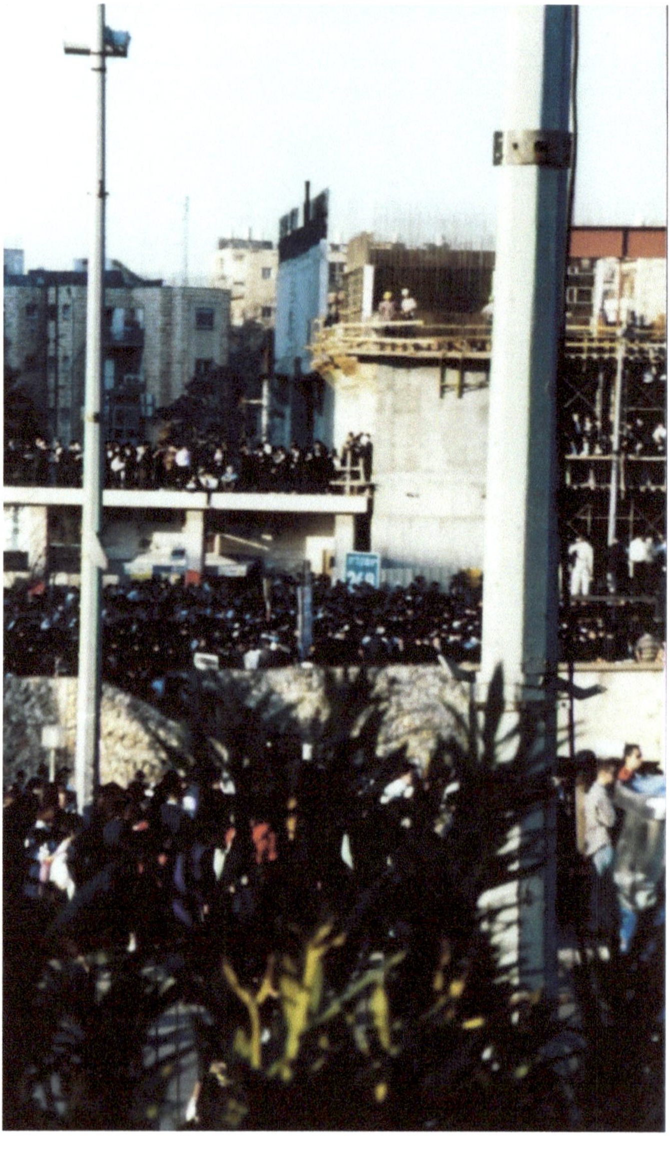

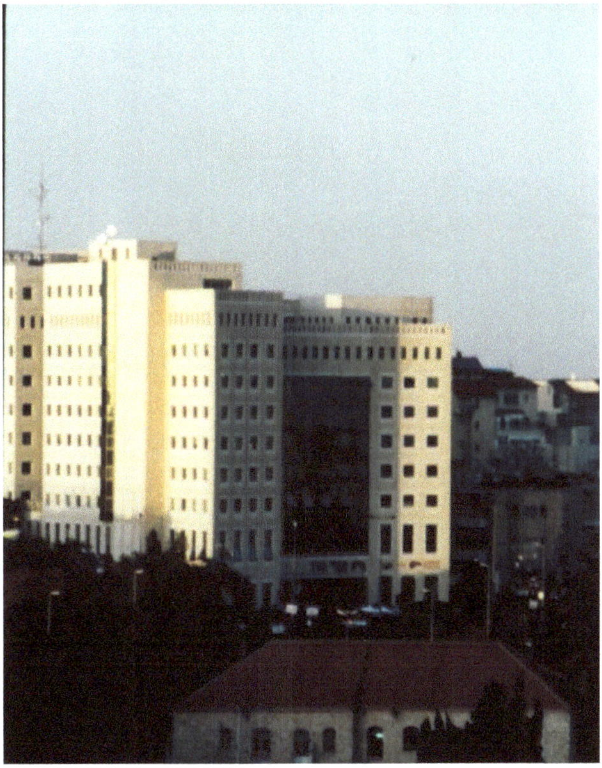

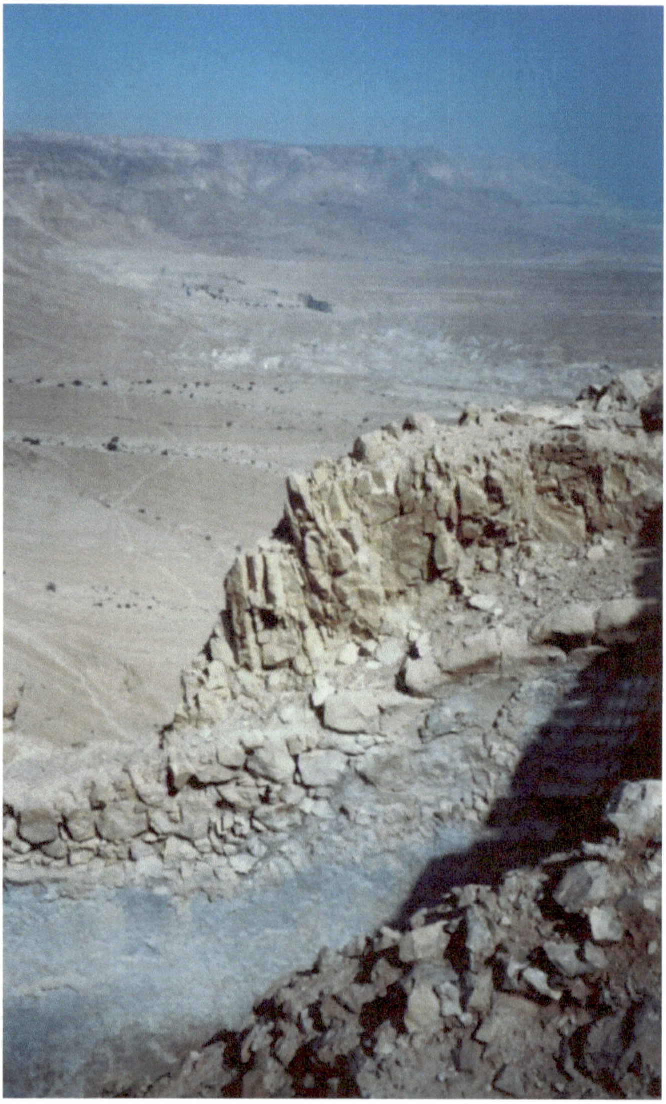

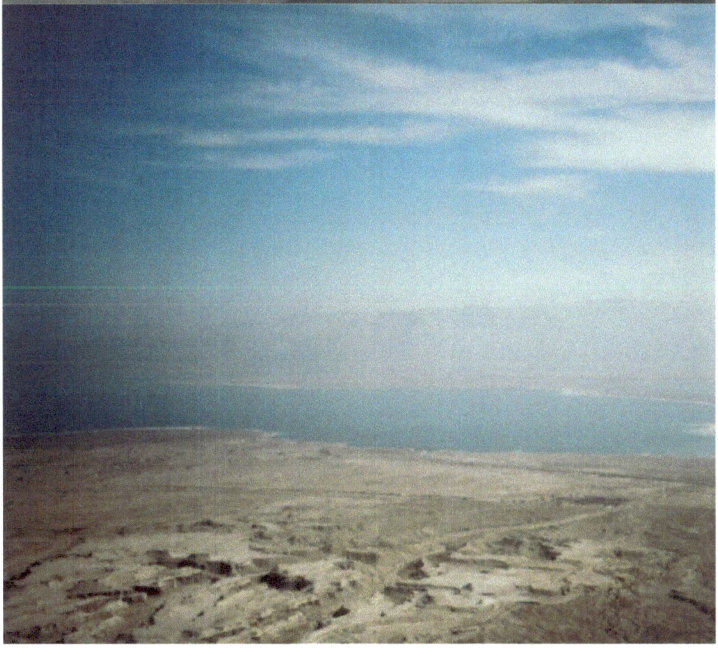

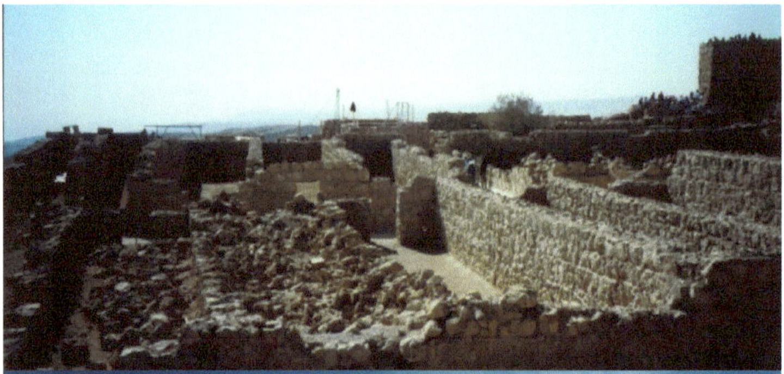
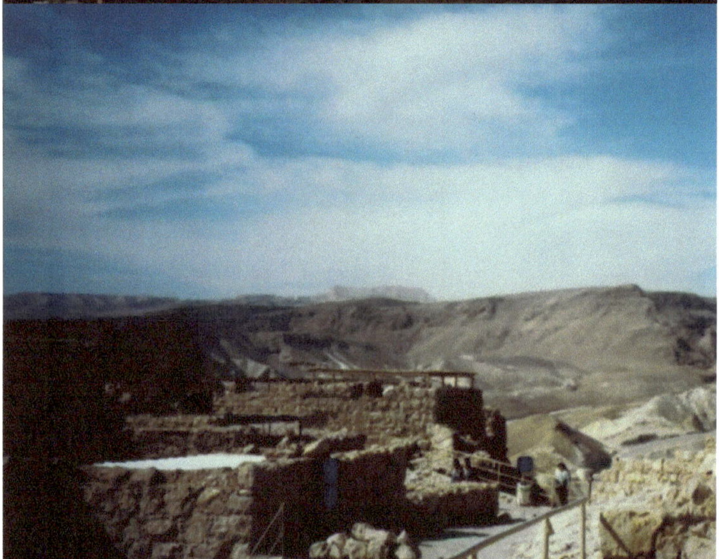

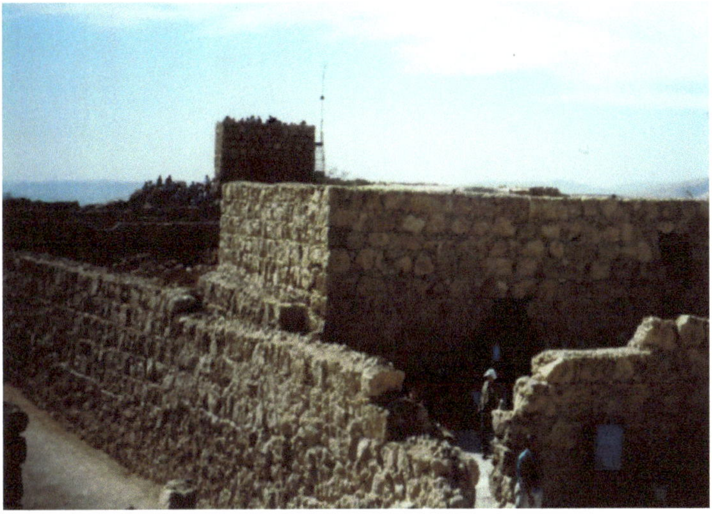

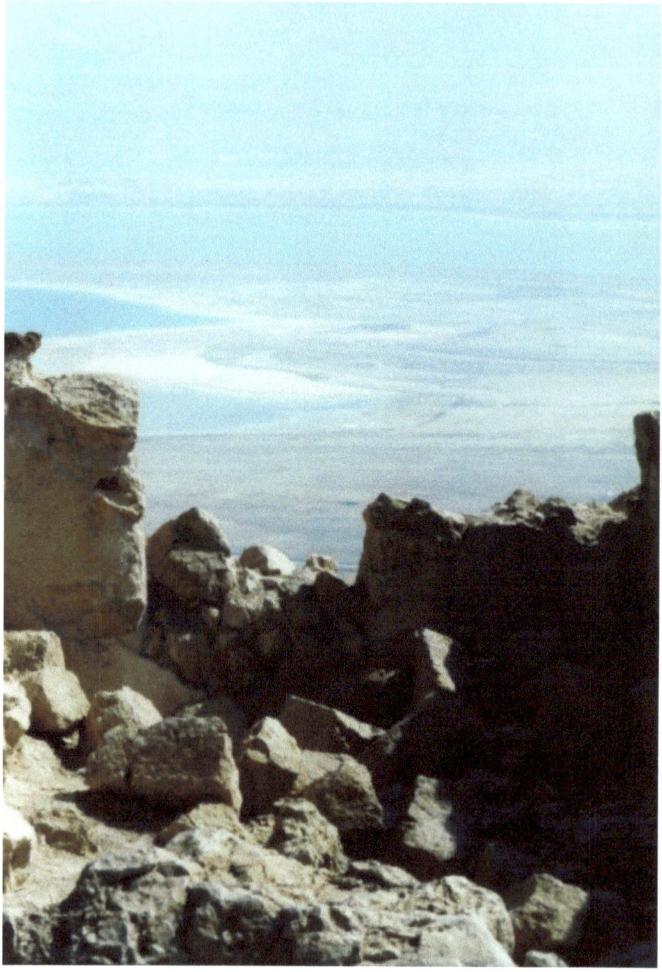

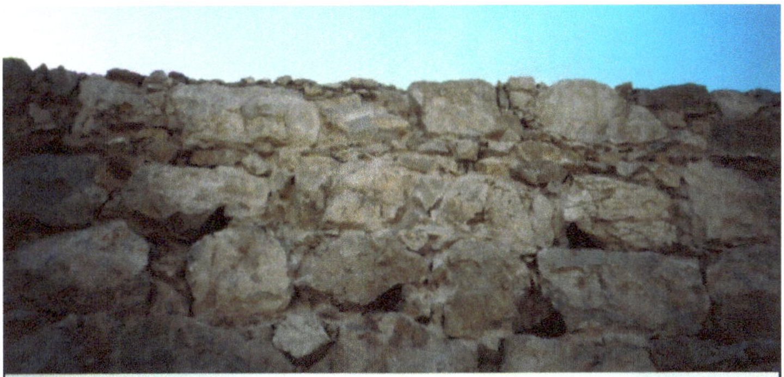

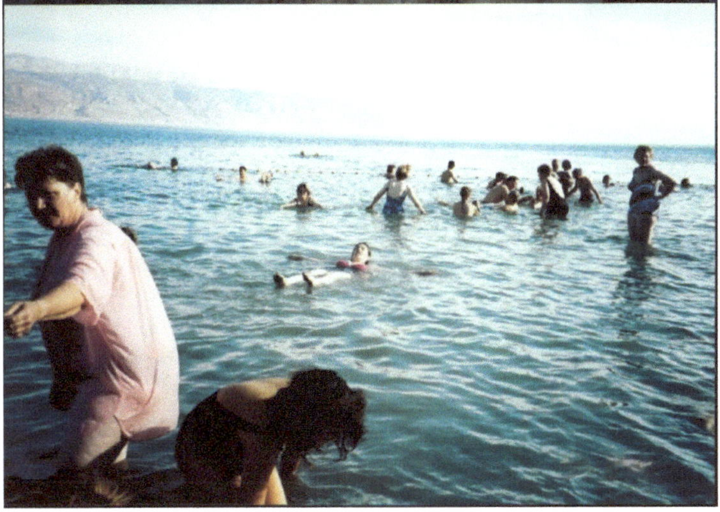

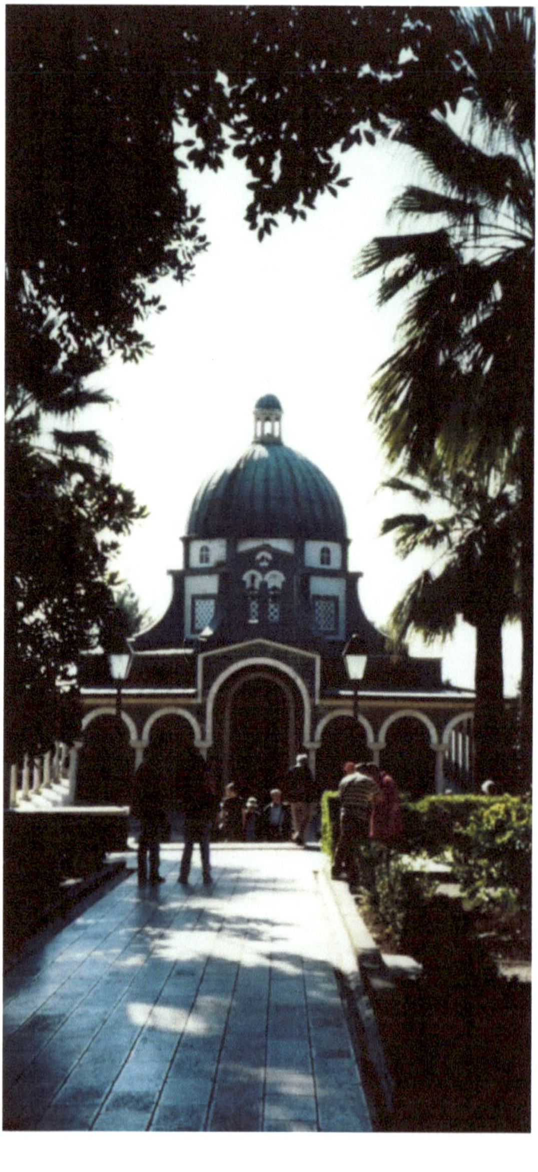

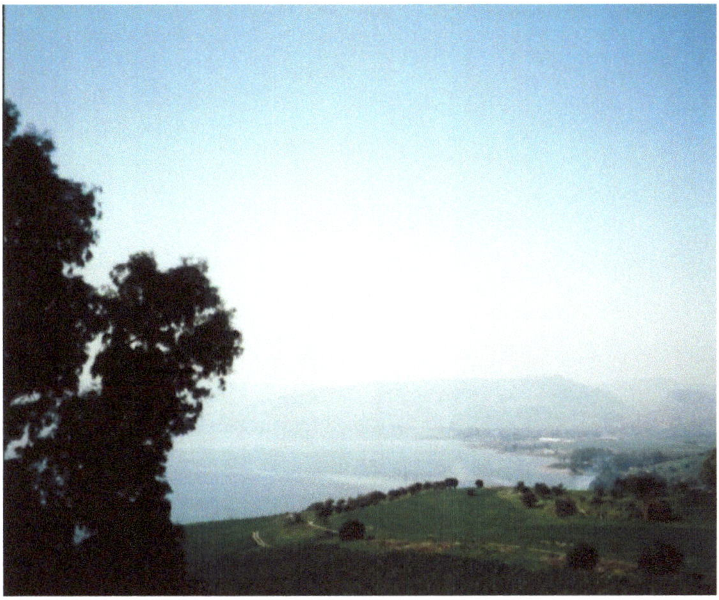

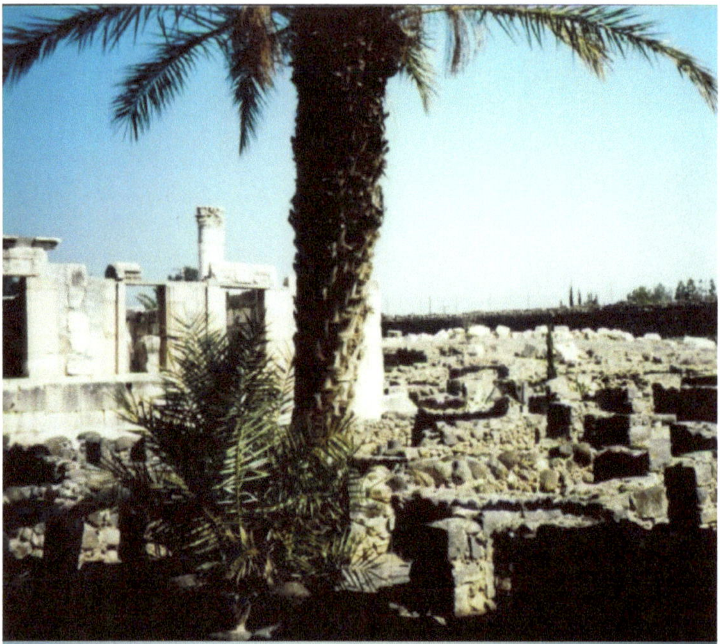

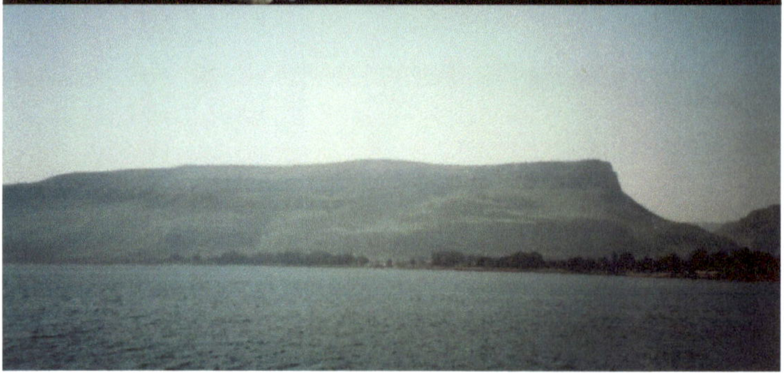

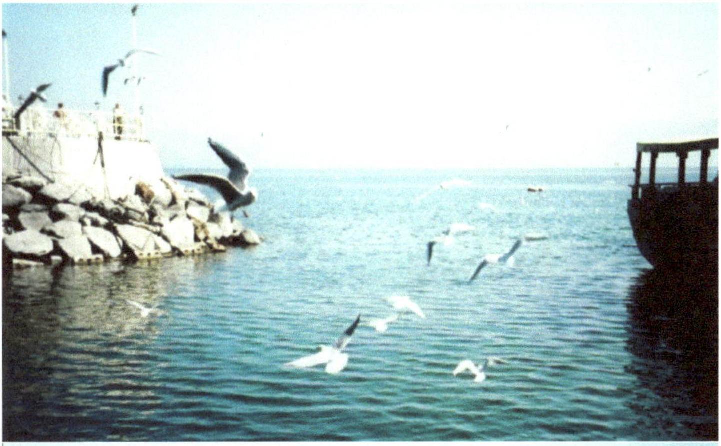

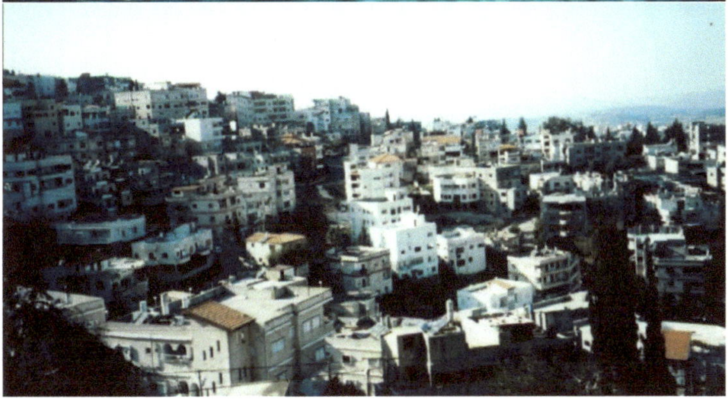

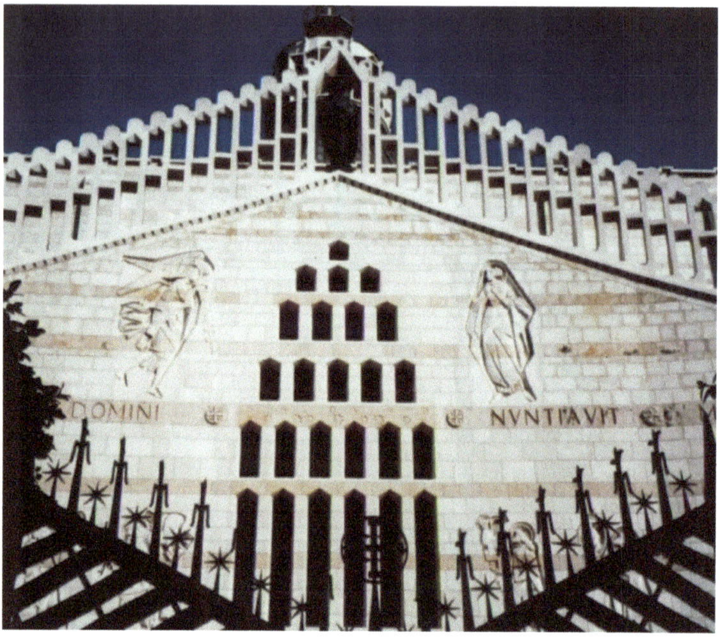
DOMINI
NVNTIAVIT

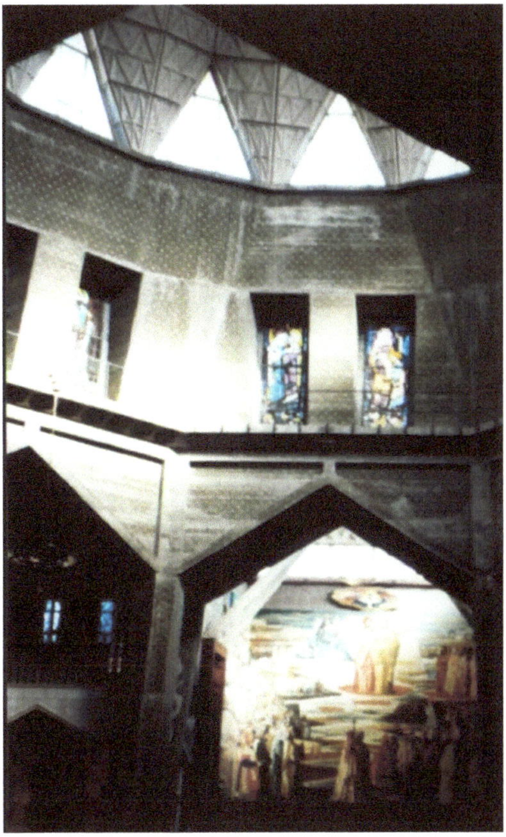

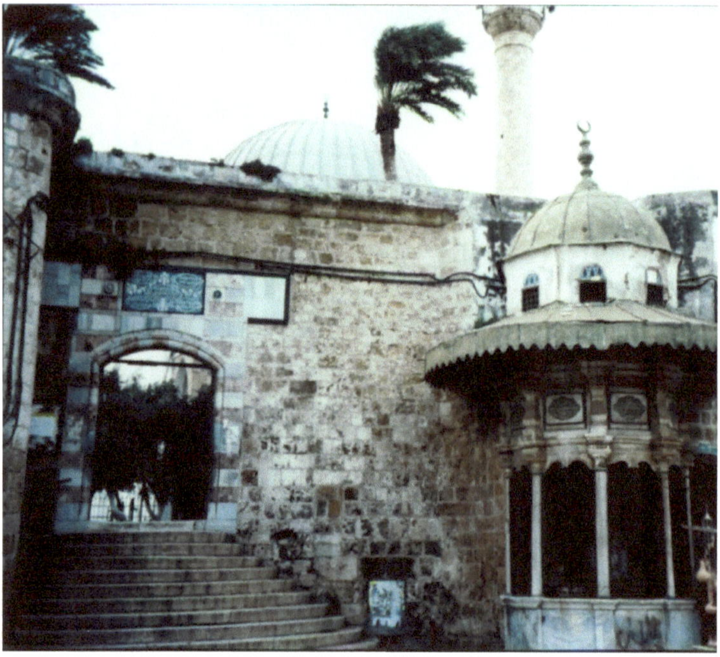

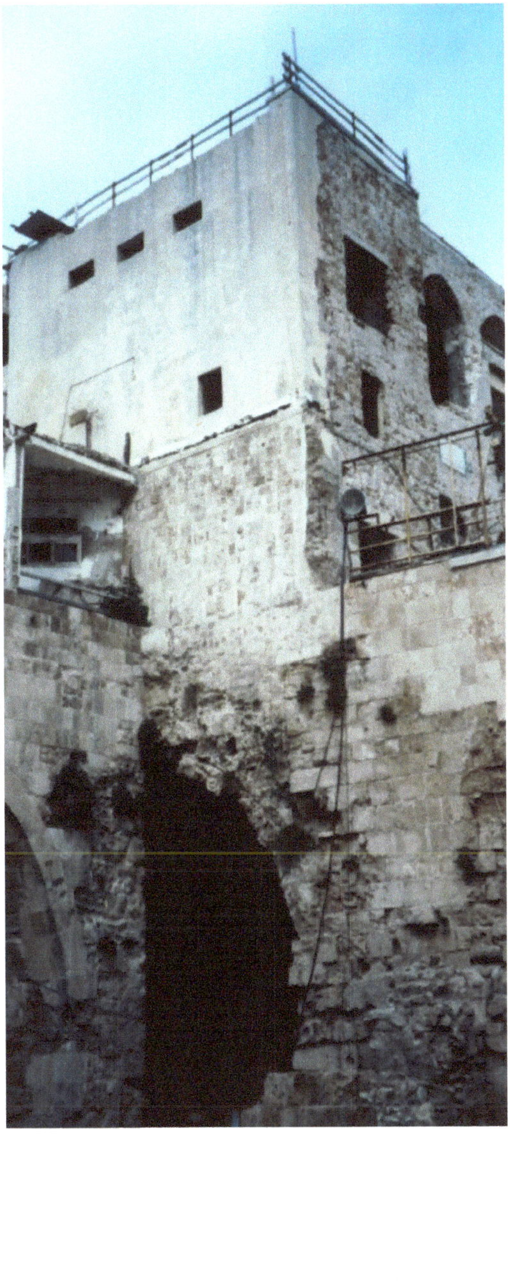

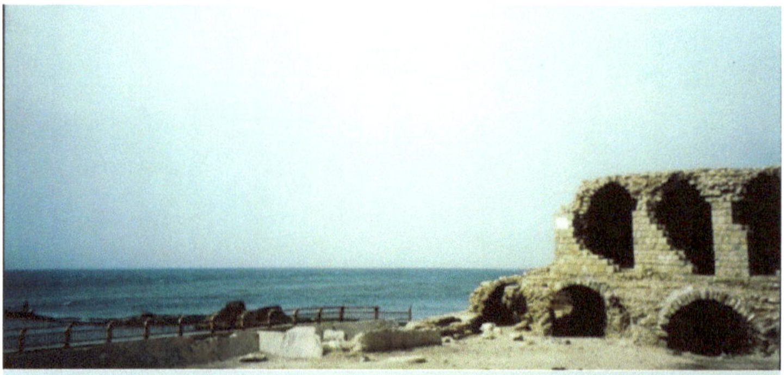

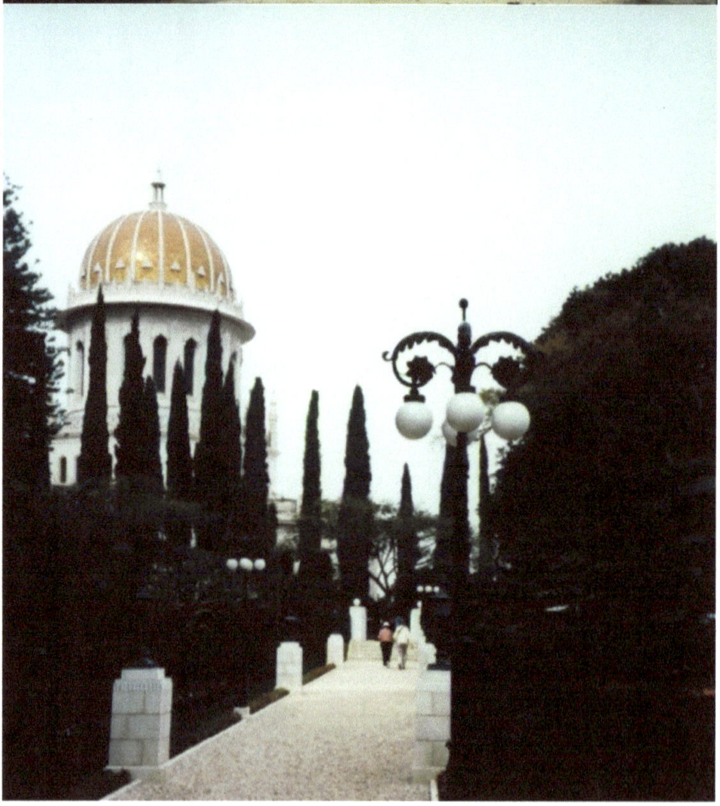

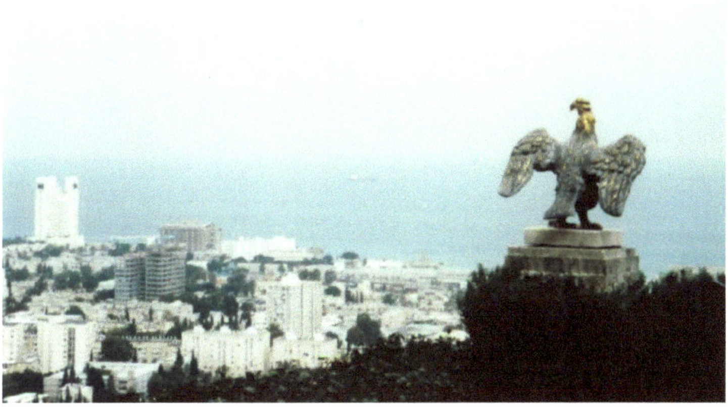

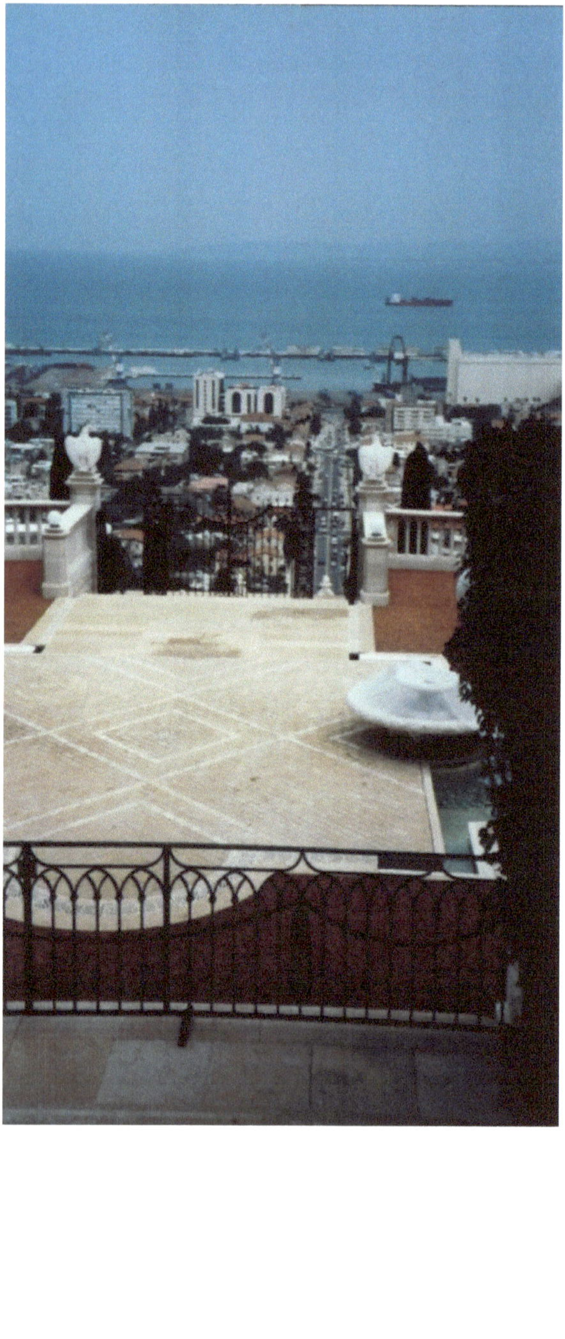

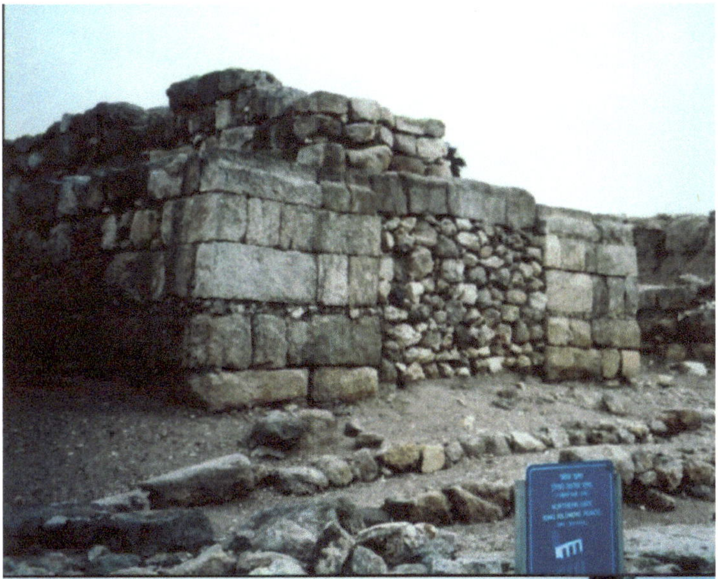

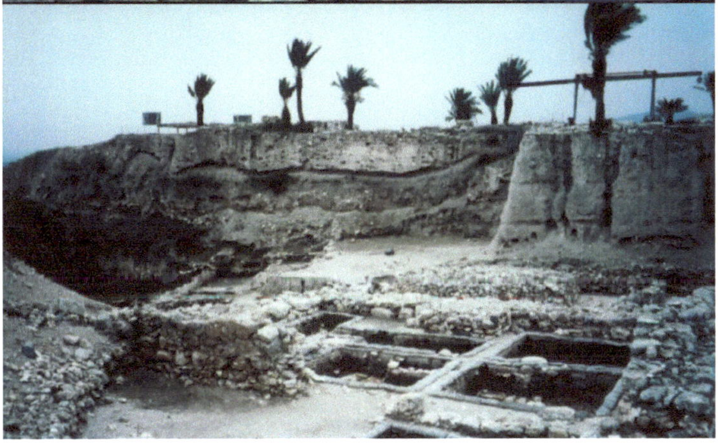

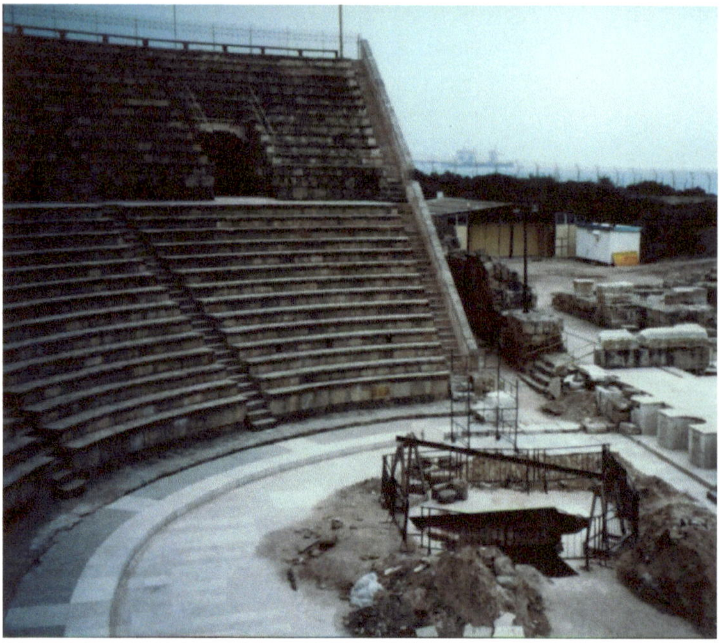

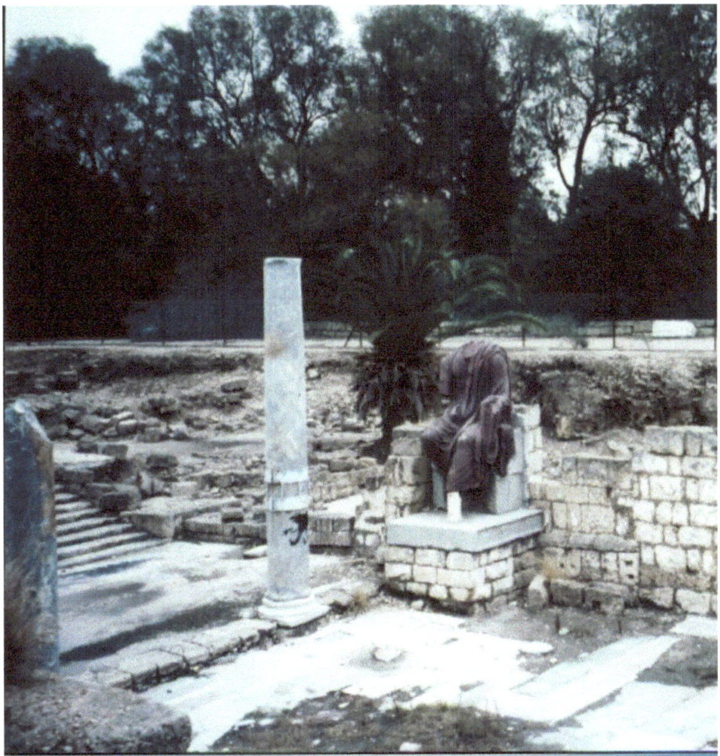

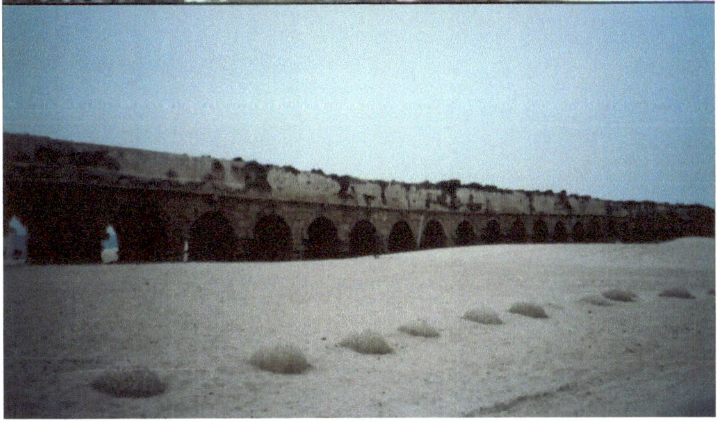

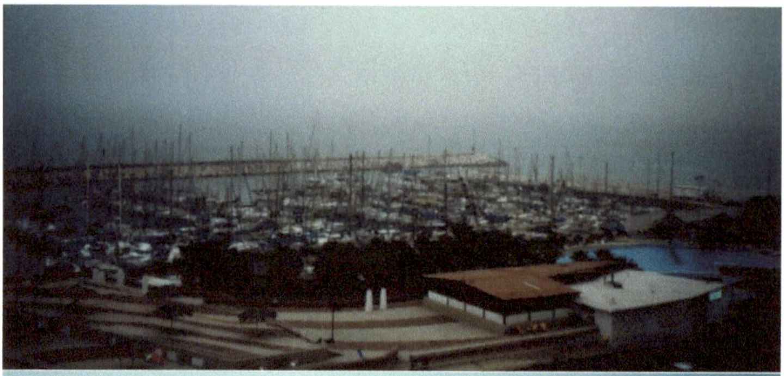

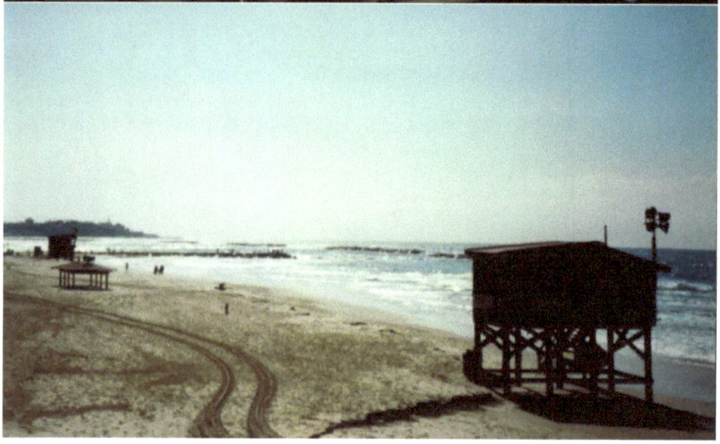

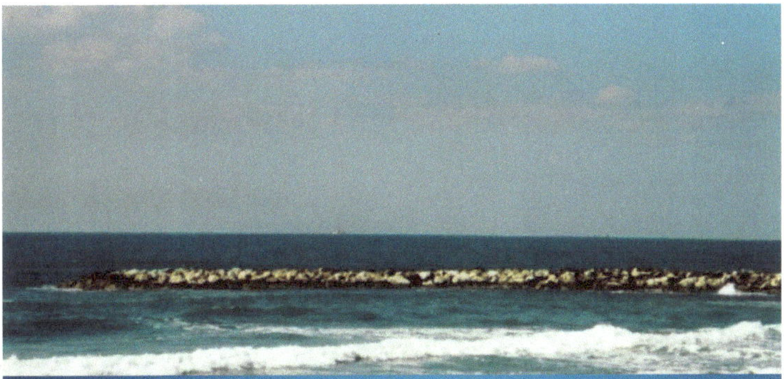

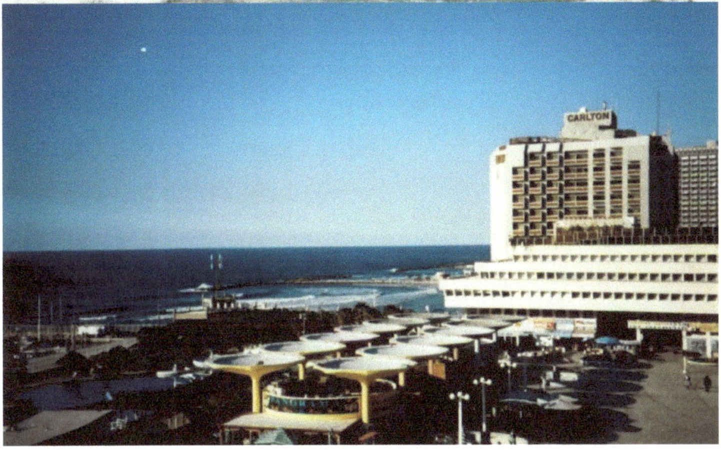
CARLTON

www.ingramcontent.com/pod-product-compliance
Lightning Source LLC
Chambersburg PA
CBHW040922180526
45159CB00002BA/580
* 9 7 8 1 5 1 4 8 8 2 0 1 6 *